Rime of the Solitary Sea Gull and Other Poems
A Celebration of Life and Love

Franklin D. Evans

PublishAmerica
Baltimore

© 2007 by Franklin D. Evans.
All rights reserved. No part of this book may be reproduced, stored in a retrieval system or transmitted in any form or by any means without the prior written permission of the publishers, except by a reviewer who may quote brief passages in a review to be printed in a newspaper, magazine or journal.

First printing

All characters in this book are fictitious, and any resemblance to real persons, living or dead, is coincidental.

At the specific preference of the author, PublishAmerica allowed this work to remain exactly as the author intended, verbatim, without editorial input.

ISBN: 1-4241-8707-9
PUBLISHED BY PUBLISHAMERICA, LLLP
www.publishamerica.com
Baltimore

Printed in the United States of America

To Betty Clayton,
whose belief in me inspired and sustained this work.

Preface

The writing of this volume was a labor of love—although labor is probably too strong a term! As most artists of my ilk, I had always written or jotted down thoughts, ideas, and sometimes even complete poems—only to have them disappear into a black hole of yesterday's news. But always there was the nagging inner voice, and sometimes outer, that I should compile these pieces into a coherent document for the purpose of eventual publication.

This book represents my finally accepting and adopting this plan, fortuitous as it was, after many years of delay and procrastination!

If I were to collect all the "scraps" of paper whereupon many of my writings died an untimely death, I'm sure many shelves of many libraries would be filled. But, just as light, nor anything else, can be retrieved from a black hole, these rantings are lost forever!

One work, which spearheaded everything else, "The Rime of the Solitary Sea Gull," was, in fact, inspired by actual forays to Lynn Beach, only to meet up with "Solomon," my pet Sea Gull each time! He grew to expect my periodic visits, and would patiently and faithfully await me. Normally, the survival instincts of animals of the wild would inhibit them from approaching within such a close proximity. Not so with Solomon. He would sit there on a rail, and listen to me as I entered his world and he mine! The story flows from there, and try as you may, you will not be able to remain in your realm once you enter that of Solomon!

Other poems in this volume similarly grab your ethos, and refuse to let it go until it has its way with you! They carry you back to the time reflected in their writing, and impart to you the pathos of the era—like it or not!

So, pack your grips, you're going on a long trip—returning a different person, indeed!

Contents

Rime of the Solitary Sea Gull 11
A Birthday Kiss 21
Atmosphere (Fuer Elena) 25
The Charge of Barbaro the Great 29
Portsmouth! 33
Midnight Train 37
Mother! 41
Out of the Darkness 45
To Claudia (If You're Still Waiting) 49
Soaring in April, Flooring in May 53
Sticks and Stones 57
The Rime of the Ancient Mainframer 61
A Day in May 67
Where Have They All Gone? 71
Would You Be a Millionaire? 75
What If? 79
Waiting in the Dark 83
Samson 87
The Benefits of Forgiveness 91
I Walked Alone 95
Admonition to Rendition 99
What Is a Valentine? 103
It's a Great Day! 107
Ode to Bobby Orr 111
Looking Back 115
She Walks in Beauty (A Sonnet for Elena) 119
To Kathy: An Erstwhile Encounter 123
Last Dance in Dedham 127
A Bad Day! 131
Street Sense 135

Unchecked Beauty	139
Queen Anne	143
The Bell Lap	147
Bermuda the Beautiful!	151
Running in Place	155
Trapped in a Time Warp	159
Frankie's House	163
Beauty!	167
Going Home Again!	171
The River Jordan	175
Seeds of Life	179
Myra, My Myra	183
Teresa's Lament (A Poem for Teresa—Who Adored Me)	187
You're Nobody 'til Somebody Wants You!	191
Whistling in the Wind	195
Giving Your All (To Frankie)	199
A Birthday Prayer for My Love	203
Long Distance Roses	207
A Valentine of Fine Wine	211
The Fan	215

Poem Number 1

Rime of the Solitary Sea Gull

The Rime of the Solitary Sea Gull

Once one day 'twas mine to stray
Upon a bird reposing
I drew e'er near, it did appear
My mien he was imploring
He sat on rail midst soothing gale
As I quiet did allure him.

It was my wont to tread this jaunt
Down by the eerie ocean
I talked his tongue, he 'peared as one
Awed as in land of Goshen!

"How strike you me, bird of the sea!"
Cried I in tones endearing
"Why sit you there, whilst far and near
The multitude is soaring?"

He turned his head, as naught was said
But all was forthwith known.
It was not meet for him to speak
He hearked my words windblown.

"You are comely, I do decree!"
He knew my thoughts 'fore said.
He met my gaze, he heard my praise
He beckoned with his head!

He knew I, too, from fellow flew
To meet, yea greet, his calling
He peered at me, as if to see
If 'deed 'twere me befalling.

He fixed his eye as I drew nigh
Directly on my soul
And thus began the dialogue
That'ere now was untold.

He cooed, I wooed, I laughed, we basked
In kindred spirits warm
"I love you, dear bird of the sea!"
He drew near fearing no harm!

He sat erect, as in reflect
On cold and clammy seawall
He shared his space—I saw God's grace
That dwells in living all.

I stretched my hand to him below
He gave a welcome nod
I asked him o'er, "why sit ye so?"
He scimmed the soggy sod.

His span was grand, his wing touched land
As he frolicked and soared in glee!
He gave a wink as wind he banked
And circled me twice three!

Communing was not taciturn,
It flowed as yon billows!
His face deep down found mine, in turn
Within my mind, yea low!

I blessed him as he talked to me
Through eyes and beak parted
He gestured toward the flowing sea
And recalled kin departed!

His eyes they told a sorry tale
As he rocked to and fro'.
He gave a wail, how filled with bale
Was this sad tale of woe!

Through eyes direct our senses met
And lingual barriers vanished
He talked to me as I were he
And oratory banished!

"My bride I took on yon grey nook
And bounteous bliss did follow
Sweet progeny therewith were three
Within that happy hollow!

"We soared and sailed, by love regaled
On each and every day!
We gave our best to every guest
Who did our nest foray!

"We taught our wee things of the sea
To navigate the shore
To use their shrift, God's given gift
To dive e'er near the floor!

"Our hearts were filled with merriment,
Our days all mays of glee.
Ne'er e'er was there cause for dissent
Nor trace of malady!

"We dined on wine of sea and Earth
We were without a lack
We fed our souls from Heaven's bowl
All cares and fears pushed back!

"Birds of Paradise were we
We crooned e'er tunes of joy!
We circumvented o'er the Sea
As if it were a toy!

"My eldest had the eyes of spies
He kept us safe, secure
He intercepted all that tried
To venture near our door!

"My middle was a jester fine
He gave us comedy
He gave us mirth from day of birth
He was my pride of three!

"My lastborn was of Earth quite skilled!
He was of letters born
His mind was eruditely filled
He did our name adorn!

"There came a mighty storm one day
Upon the mighty ocean
My kith forthwith did not dismay
Distress was but a notion!

"The wind, the rain from Northeast came
It rendered flying futile
It came in thrusts and mighty gusts
The sea soared like the Nile!

"The dreary dread of this tempest
Was felt for four furlongs!
The matted down did cause to drown
The mean of Vesper's throng!

"They wist not where to part the air
They could nor lead nor follow
They flew His path, blind faith to dare
To find their beloved hollow!

"Ten thousand times the flock entwined
To damp this raging beast!
They fought the rain and died in vain
In searching for the East!

"The sky was black, our Light a lack
As Hell did rain below!
We were attacked by lifeless packs
As though shot by crossbow!

"The very sky did lend an eye
To sigh a sorry din!
Yea, water cleansed the stench of death
But none can heal within!

"A blackness came upon the Earth
As locusts in land of Pharaoh
I wondered loud if this were birth
Of time when Time was no more!

"The sandy shore was pure no more
It was of life devoid!
My four I implored along the floor
I knelt down 'fore the Lord!

"I wept in tune, with the vast dunes
Of lifeless forms, I pray!
I cannot burn, nor e'en spurn
The thoughts unto this day!

"The floor was covered o'er, I wist
The list could not be known
The spirits from these noble kith
Had mercifully flown!

"The hallowe'ed moon did shine eftsoon
It gave an eerie sight!
Yea, ghosts and goons gave chase to whom
Rose up out of the night!

"They all aghast with one last gasp
Raised up, "Dear God!" from under!
And then as quick they did remit
Their souls 'midst claps of thunder!

This sorrowful state seized all save one
He was by Mercy spared!
The siege is done, his bride and sons
Will no more grace their lair!

It was the first of Harvest last
That I saw Solomon
It was just then that he did spin
This tale of woe upon!

I chanced to see him yet again
Today in bleak December
I said within, "I'll see my friend!"
And lo, he did remember!

He circled low, he circled high
He circled all around!
He playfully set sail at me
I fell upon the ground!

It was I knew a last salute
From wondrous Solomon
I am enriched to have witnessed
His presence, as the Sun!

He sits there now, with furrowed brow
On that cold and clammy seawall!
I see God's eye within him cry
It touches each and all!

We are one plan, by God's own hand
Drawn up similarly
We love, we cry, we live, we die
We go back to the sea!

As I recede, I feel him bleed
I feel him sadden o'er!
"I'll see thee, friend, down by the Sea!"
I see his face no more!

Poem Number 2

A Birthday Kiss

A Birthday Kiss

It's been a while, I do surmise, since first we came to view
But o'er the years, through toil and tears, ne'er sight was lost of you
I do aver, naught o'er this earth, shall sever the sight of you!

The years have brought, what many have sought, but found by just a few
Sweet, swooshing tides of Ocean's rides, mind's nectar and honeydew
It brings sweet pain to once again wist wisp was dearly you!

But on this day, He's blessed you way beyond that many can say
I pray the love, flowered by Above, will present you this array
Of love and kisses and birthday wishes, as many I can convey!

As travel we may on life's highway, we'll pause to reminisce
Of love's first bloom, and then, eftsoon, the bliss of our first kiss
I loved you then, I love you now, I've loved you ever since!

Poem Number 3

Atmosphere (Fuer Elena)

Atmosphere (Fuer Elena)

Few be there, who can charge the air
Simply by strolling in
Fewer still, who can, at will
Light up whither she's been!

I cannot recall, anyone at all
Whose aura opens eyes and mien
Like yours! I aver, and others concur
Your gaze unlocks a wall!

So in the end, I need not bend,
To see if you are there
I feel your lilt, ere eyes are tilt
Your atmosphere is here!

One can't resist, like light, I wist
And flag of Guinevere!

Poem Number 4

The Charge of Barbaro the Great

The Charge of Barbaro the Great

"The sun shines bright on my old Kentucky home!"
Wrote Stephen Foster long ago
Little did he know
That at the time
He was writing the rhyme
That would unveil and hail the King and his court
As he pranced and danced in a life so short!

Dear Barbaro, we hardly knew you!
And now we lift a glass to you
We toast your stately legs
Which brilliantly pegged
The standards of excellence!

Your amiable nature was life unfurled
Your indomitable spirit infected the World!
Vanquishing *that* infection
Like so many foes that fell before!

Run, Barbaro, run! Proud colt and fast!
Down the stretch of the Valley of Death!
Run with the six-hundred of yon Light Brigade
As the mighty men and their mounts
Stared down dour Death
As you did, dear pride of best!

Soar on, noble Barbaro! Soar!
Crash the gates once more
That separates seraphins
From mortal men!

Thunder on, sweet Barbaro, and valiant
Thrice-crowned prince, of Mercurial bent!
We *will* not forget, we *cannot* relent
Your mind-numbing charge into Earthly lore,
Yea, evermore!

Poem Number 5

Portsmouth!

Portsmouth!

It's as if you've left all that is your own
To enter another Time zone!
It's as if you've kissed her mouth—
The beautiful, beguiling Portsmouth!

Your breath comes more quickly, your eyes twice as twinkly—
The closer you are to her touch!
You feel her embrace you, as nigh she will face you—
The beautiful, beguiling Portsmouth!

I came to enjoy her, yea love and adore her
The beautiful, beguiling Portsmouth!
You cannot be bored there—your spirits will soar there
The beautiful, beguiling Portsmouth!

When first I approached her, she stirred me down deep!
I fancied I'd traveled to heav'n in my sleep!
She gives you such eros, you cannot retreat!
The beautiful, beguiling Portsmouth!

I hobnobbed the masses 'midst projects and classes
In this kingly, majestic domain!
You cannot abstain, you'll forever remain
In the beautiful, beguiling Portsmouth!

It mellowed with me—it gave Liberty
The beautiful, beguiling Portsmouth!
The feeling was grand, when I held her hand!
The beautiful, beguiling Portsmouth!

It grew even more, when I tallied the score
And felt it Mutual!
I cannot e'en feign, I cannot disdain
The beautiful, beguiling Portsmouth!

It grew with us, I saw the cusp
Of vile and doughty distrust!
But through it all, I heard her call
The beautiful, beguiling Portsmouth!

I stand here now near midship's bow
Awaiting my grand return!
Ne'er e'er will I leave, ne'er e'er will I spurn
The beautiful, beguiling Portsmouth!

Poem Number 6

Midnight Train

Midnight Train

It had started ever so slowly its relentless run to River's mouth
The worn trials and trails keeping unwavering course
The rails were white-hot from the daily distant discourse—
Of unplanned visits and junkets—always due south!

The churning of the locomotive kept perfect pitch!
It whistled down the tracks near barrier speed!
It was competing unknowingly 'gainst time and deed—
It was trying desperately to keep destiny with Hour of Witch!

In tune with this streaking, strident harbinger of doom
Another part of the world was reverberating, pulsating—
The magnet of mind had foretold it, ere the sonic boom
Which would fill the air, where two parties were relating.

If it was not known then, then certainly it is known now!
"Was that for me?" came the sudden enthralling entreaty.
Scarce was I aware of her presence there—
So that, indeed, was an impossibility!

Unbeknownst to me, she had boarded that train—in a rush
Carried cruelly there by whim of circumstance!
We tried desperately to arrest its unrelenting dance
But it began, as planned, without us!

Poem Number 7

Mother

Mother!

I don't remember, but this is what they say—
They say she ran through Hell—well down the lattice
To stand on the ledge, the edge of Eternity!
She challenged Death and won—both for herself and her son!

Fire in front of her! Fire in back of her!
Fire to the top of her! Fire under her feet!
This did not stop her onslaught—her quest to defeat
The Grim One, desperate to deter!

She leveled a blockade of well-wishers there
Attempting to interdict her flight!
Try though they might
They grabbed vainly at air!

She was deep into the bowels of perdition
When the object of her frantic foray appeared.
With bravery that defied both fire and dire—
She wrested him from His clammy clutches—unseared!

As I sit and stare now at image of her
She was a mere babe, herself, of eighteen!
She is cuddling her pride and joy and beaming—
Seemingly relating her heroic story to camera!

No one knows the throes of a mother intent
No one knows the courage of a mother on bent
Hear well then all ye that read herein—
The story has not been told—barely braced to begin!

Poem Number 8

Out of the Darkness

Out of the Darkness

In the darkness I scarce can see
But the Lord has His hands on me!
In the darkness though I fret—
The Lord's will is always met!
Because we love Him day to day
The Lord will *always* make a way!
In the darkness, light takes flight
But the Lord *never* leaves—He is *ever* our sight!
Day by day, His will be done—
Our God reigns on—though day is done!

Poem Number 9

To Claudia (If You're Still Waiting)

To Claudia (If You're Still Waiting)

Claudia, remember the rendezvous with Jane and you
At Father's that fateful day?
It was in the seventies, and oh how heavenly
It was when you looked my way!

Sweet and fair were you that night
Deep and daring were your eyes, ever bright!
The conversation lilted and lollied away
I could tell something special was hap'ning straightaway!

It was hardly the lap of luxury—peanut shells on the floor!
As we exchanged acquaintance, we wanted more! More!
As we swilled with delight, further on into the night,
We reasoned that this was a repeatable sight!

We drew ever nearer—no newness alarm
Came to us, as we imbibed our deepening charm!
It became known during our dapper discourse
That we set pen to paper on a volume of source.

We sang, we danced, we strolled, we pranced
'Til Time had fritted away!
You looked at your watch, and then your clock
And said, "Whither the words will we say?"

It was a thought that squarely had caught
Me thoroughly unaware!
I replied, with candor, "When the book is bought!"
Which now is in prepare!

Well, my Claudia, if still you're on Beacon
I know you're not now holding a beacon
For me—after all, many years have passed!
Does that flame yet endure? Was not cruel Time a cure?

Where'er you may be today, Claudia—this is for you!
It comes with all the love and fond memories singularly past due!
When you read this, Claudia, you may not help but know
My thoughts are still with you—may'st love ever grow!

Poem Number 10

Soaring in April, Flooring in May

Soaring in April, Flooring in May

Frankie was right when he talked about Life—
Soaring in April, flooring in May!
To note the balance 'tween rice and strife—
Soaring in April, flooring in May!

It seems to arrive in pairs, I wist
Soaring in April, flooring in May!
You score in one.—you get the jist!
Soaring in April, flooring in May!

Chief of all Northeast, at once!
Soaring in April, flooring in May!
Now they won't hire you as a dunce!
Soaring in April, flooring in May!

Controlling all of Company
Soaring in April, flooring in May!
Now they offer you coffee for a fee!
Soaring in April, flooring in May!

Rejecting one hundred by the year
Soaring in April, flooring in May!
Now, no money for a beer!
Soaring in April, flooring in May!

Pursued relentless by the fair kind
Soaring in April, flooring in May!
Now a glance brings you askance!
Soaring in April, flooring in May!

Faster than a flash, an Olympian dash
Soaring in April, flooring in may!
Now, oh drat! You're hailing a cab!
Soaring in April, flooring in May!

If ever April should revisit, I aver
Soaring in April, flooring in May!
We'll know whither May, we'll seize the day!
Soaring in April, flooring in May!

Poem Number 11

Sticks and Stones

Sticks and Stones

Sticks and stones will break your bones
Whoever said reverse?
But words and tones and rants and moans
Will grow a gruesome curse!

The edicts of the wisest one,
Solomon, soliloquys—
He states that on mandate of tongue
Life lives or Death decrees!

Yes, we stand staunchly at the helm
As ship pulls out from harbor
We launch into another realm
Words winged with ire or ardor!

When this is done, Angelic ones
Dispatch to heed your call!
It matters not if words are fraught
With love or vitriol!

Listen, dear ones, and do not besmirch—
Almighty declared it so!
The Celestial Laws of physics, the First:
Where words lead, deeds will follow!

Poem Number 12

Rime of the Ancient Mainframer

The Rime of the Ancient Mainframer

It is an ancient Mainframer
And he stoppeth one of three
'Pray verify and verily,
Wherefore stopp'st thou me?'

"There was a wayward vacuum
When Time was very new
It coughed and spat; Alas and Alack!
It gave the sum of two!

"Sweet progeny of EAM, it was
It lugged a heavy load
From Hollerith to punched-card bliss
His tale he did unfold!

"It was a soggy night, I wist
In traipsing by the Bridge
I came upon the Behemoth one
On yon technology ridge!

"'Twas in New Ark of the War
Where 'gan this turbulent trek
Where suckling science forayed forth
'Midst drums and runs and decks!

"Forsooth, we were as souls in church
We were by this quite stunned!
Ne'er once at work was speed besmirched
So sleek was Univac's son!

"He strained to entertain the bits
And bytes coaxed quickly in
His hum was steady, he stayed at ready
May'st hear the rattling din!

"As data oozed through Reader's view
It gave a rhythmic roar
Magnetic core was filled in o'er
The merry, melodious hue!

"A solitary mag tape spun
Like Cyclops, I aver!
It mesmerized the novice one
Useless to resist her!

"It factored fast the mean and class
Of data deftly entered!
It threw the stats a forward pass
And plotted them dead center!

"Sweet calculus or abacus
Was oft sequentially offered
If, perchance, parlance disrupts
An alternate was proffered!

"The program decks devoured thus
Gave life to mind's design
Cerebrum sent a mighty pulse
As thought and deed aligned!

"Experimental masonry
Drew Future within grasp
Variances and analyses
Do loops like lightning, fast!

"To crowded boardrooms decked in best
Came reams of thought encoded
All answers shown at aught behest
As new delights unfolded!

"He gave a bow for deed well done
And praise cascades eftsoon
His breast he beat,'twas no mean feat
He felt at feast bridegroom!

"Alas! Daresay! Came Y2K
Like thugs in ninety-nine
They stole the bride, how minions cried!
And hied to History's pine!

"The meeting light grows dim tonight
As Past recedes from view
The bride is old, the groom has told
This tale since thousand-two!

"As dusk relentless does befall
The Ancient One, forlorn
Is exiting the hallowe'ed halls
To 'pare the 'morrow morn!

Poem Number 13

A Day in May

A Day in May

What is so gay as a day in may
When warblers chronicle and croon?
The storm abates, and joy awaits
Summer's sun and fun eftsoon!

What is so nigh as a day in July
When Nature has longsince shed its gloom!
Her once ice-crusted eyelids blink alluringly
As a bride awaiting her groom.

When vows, long abandoned, are renewed
When new nests are merrily made
When the robin beats boldly his red breast
And sings to the Heavens his happy serenade!

What is so royal as a rhyme in tune
Sung beauteously, 'fusively 'neath an adorning moon!
When sparkling brooks reflect night's bright
In meandering meadows, awaiting daylight!

What is so beautiful as a butterfly in flight
When winter's cuccoon has been shed with delight!
When earth has loosed its hold on mirth
And birds return to roost from search!

What is so alluring as the ocean, churning
Visiting our yearnings with not aught to say?
What is so inspiring as a desire, burning
To live all our days in the month of May!

Poem Number 14

Where Have They All Gone?

Where Have They All Gone?

I took for granted they'd always be there!
Where? Oh where have they gone?
From fool to school, didn't think they'd dare
To leave me all alone!

They were there for me when I first won the prize
They were there when I ascended the highest heights
They were there with me when the middle was made
They were there with me when adolescence faded.

They were there when we made a quarter on the dollar
They were there when everyone gave a hoot and a holler!
They were there when our future began to unfold
They were there when we sailed past the quarter pole!

They were there when we enjoyed our sophomore hop
They were there all night, doing the Beebop and slop!
We were all together at the junior prom—
We were all together when love came along!

We were together again, for one final fling
We were together when we gathered our teen-age toys!
We were together when we finally exited the ring
We were together when we took our bittersweet bows!

We pursued careers that flung us far
The first we knew—here we are!
Our poker game has so downsized
We're losing to life one at a time!

And now as we iterate over the list
We scarce can place anyone, I wist!
I wonder and ponder, from moon to sun—
Where are they now? Where have they gone?

Poem Number 15

Would You Be a Millionaire?

Would You Be a Millionaire?

Would you be a millionaire,
and all your riches declare?
Or would you aspire to something higher
And teach to treat men fair?

Would you pursue, rather than rue
the chance to "strike it rich"?
Would you imbue your final clue
To avoid that dastardly ditch?

When life's long shot promises a pot
And instant riches and fame
When success beckons with siren thoughts
Would you hie to hear her name?

When bartering on life's vapid stages
Chattel avails very little
You may buy with endless wages—
A fiddle, a faddle, and a kettle!

I, dear World, would shun all this
For mind's wealth, health sublime—
For love and bliss and midsummer's kiss
Until the end of Time!

Poem Number 16

What If?..............

What If?…………..

Our main indulgence—truth be told
Is what might have happened, ere we're old!
It gnaws and claws, and baits and dates
it will not pause'til sweet sleep abates!

It taunts and daunts and castigates
It jaunts and stomps and permeates
Our every thought when things unseal:
"Why did you this, you imbecile!"

Had you done that instead of this
Your life, perchance, would be one big kiss!
Had pride and greed not made you miss
Innumerable nights might be shared in bliss!

What if….I had answered that phone?
What if….I hadn't gone alone?
What if….I had taken that job?
Oh my God! I think I've been robbed!

Poem Number 17

Waiting in the Dark

Waiting in the Dark

Have you ever waited for something—
Waiting in the dark?
Have you ever waited for someone—
Waiting in the park?

They seem, indeed, to suspend Time
Earth's order seems strangely out of rhyme!
Your grip on Destiny compromised
Your thoughts meander undisguised!

The reasons for these ramblings are clear:
You do not know if unknowns will present,
You do not know if plans will consent,
You do not know—Oh dear! The fear!

But—when joyous appearance is achieved
When uncertainties have been unceremoniously relieved,
Life is retrieved back from the abyss!
And mirth and lark embrace with a kiss!

Poem Number 18

Samson

Samson

Listen! My children, old and young
You'll hear the story of the svelte Samson
You'll hear of strength and love supreme
You'll hear of how he's been redeemed!

Wheree'er he was—on air or ground
Always 'twas good that could be found.
Always 'twas self that disappeared
Always 'twas love and goodness shared!

From humble beginnings on Virginia's farms
To far-flung places, like Vietnam
Samson showed both strength and might
Samson's ally was God and Right!

His life is as spectacled as a flag unfurled
His influence is felt half 'round the world!
He learned well The Lord's living rules
He lives the life—he's paid his dues!

After many victories and few defeats
He felt therewith still incomplete
As told in Bible, strength and might
Took flight on wings on Delilah's sight!

Delilah did what heretofore
Was done in dreams, nothing more!
She took his strength, from locks ungloved
And wreaked him weak with consummate love!

Together they waxed strong and fervent
Bound always together by Holy covenant
A sweet shoulder for his head to lay
'Delilah', dare say, is the beautiful Verne'!

Poem Number 19

The Benefits of Forgiveness

The Benefits of Forgiveness

If you pursue vengeance,
hatred, and malice
Your enemies have succeeded
In hurting you twice!

Because they have struck
The wound and fled
While you're still stuck
On what's done and said!

Forgive and forget
The dastardly deed
Give it to God
And move on instead!

He will purge the pain
And slight you were dealt
He will scourge the disdain
That you might have felt!

Thus saith The Lord
From beginning of Time
Lest ye forthwith fall
"Vengeance is mine!"

Poem Number 20

I Walked Alone

I Walked Alone

Her voice was always haunting to me
Hauntingly beautiful!
Her eyes were always daunting to me
Dauntingly inscrutable!

Mona's match! No less the praise
Her piercing gaze illuminates days!
Where e'er you stand the feel will follow
Try though you can, the deed is hollow

It pervades the inner and outer One
Until you find yourself alone
Flowered by her Sun!
I walked alone—ere day was done!

Escorted solely by Centurion Cherubs
That gave importuned passage to her world.
I saw the teeming crowd shrink violet-like away
As I walked alone that day—flowered by her face!

Poem Number 21

Admonition to Rendition

Admonition to Rendition

If there were no down
There would be no up!
If there were no clowns
There would be no circus!

When whence come things
Becomes apparent
When whistler's rings
Blocks ducats and carats

When long range lands
And jolts your rack
When stiff right hands
Land you on your back

Never! Never prone alone!
Hurry! Scurry afoot!
Get going! Deliver one
That renders all else moot!

Then, when tables reverse
And you've annulled attrition
Albeit terse:
It was your rendition!

Poem Number 22

What Is a Valentine?

What Is a Valentine?

A valentine, if I may opine
Is savory, like fine, sweet wine
It gives a lift to all around
It is a gift, with love unbound

What is a valentine, you ask
It is the warmth of the sun in bask
It illuminates the darkest days
Existence thrives on its radiant rays

All this and more I can assure
Describes its meaning—love and allure
But the dearest description that I can find
Is that this Valentine is mine!

Poem Number 23

It's a Great Day!

It's a Great Day!

If you can feel it, you can seal it!
If you can say 'Great Day',
You've initiated a confession—
The bane of our naturalized expression!
Indeed! We provide daily intercession

For those souls sickened from life
Seeking respite from stress and strife,
Looking back at the nearly complete canvas
They have brushed—hesitating before applying
the finishing touches.

They extend their grateful grasp to us
And we lock arms in love
Snatching them from the precipitous clutches
Of self-designed resignation!

As manic mornings melt into active afternoon
And day's gloom looms—
If you have aided one soul,
You have made it a great day
For all mankind!

Poem Number 24

Ode to Bobby Orr

Ode to Bobby Orr

I remember Ronnie asking me, "Ever hear of this guy?"
That was a score and many scores ago.
"He's going to be great, you know!"
Little did she know!

Nothing, or no one like you had dared daunt the Rocket
Or Tiny or Maury or Belliveau!
Howe, now standing in the limelight of your legacy
Your greatness seems to rise from the pages of history!

Already you were in a different strata!
And hardly had you even begun the battle
Or llluminated our homes with electric evenings—
with your brilliance, bravado and talent!

Bobby, as I watched you rush headlong
From end to end
I swear I saw a Red-winged Hawk
Lay back and gawk in mesmerized awe!
Not believing what he saw!

Never, in annals, was there one brilliant to the core
as the Fabulous, Flashy, Number Four!
Once, in yesteryear, amid an incredulous sigh,
I blinked in wonderment—I even saw you *fly*!

Fred could hardly contain his glee!
He *screamed* in crescendo, so enthralled was he!
The raucous Garden *rocked* to the core
The rink was sinking—from the roar of adore!

The crowd has long since exited
these magical doors—
But should you listen intently to the walls
You can still hear Fred's breathless call—
"Score!!!!!!!!—Bobby Orr!!!!!!!!"

Poem Number 25

Looking Back

Looking Back

I looked back—and it was nineteen seventy-one
It was a noteworthy time—life living in rhymes(sometimes).
It was a time of self-creation, elevation, loving and fun
Scarce it appears one decade—no less four and one!
It was a time of jousting the world head-on!
Victory 'most e'er foregone
Battles—yea wars—wonderfully won!

I looked back—and it was nineteen eighty-five
Green seemed the dream taught us—and true!
No one could derail this express headed for bliss!
The lantern hung high—the memory of your kiss!

I looked back—and it was nineteen ninety-five
Earthbound Concorde carrying cadres of materiele
Streaking westward towards the setting sun!
The eager station had met us halfway—

Journey's end—anon fare to pay!
Alas! And alack!
We must reverse track!
And head home straight away!

I looked back—and it was two thousand and one
We had quietly passed into Christ's third term.
Oh how we yearned for those bold and haughty days
Where the rays of our Candle never parted us!

Many a day we had not one ray
To gently stroke or start us!
I saw you waving your lantern on the platform
As we approached for a landing
The bristling' of the brakes seemed to be exclaiming,
"Welcome home!"

Poem Number 26

She Walks in Beauty

She Walks in Beauty
(A Sonnet for Elena)

As you lilt and tilt your head
As you glow and flow through aisles
As you meander 'round with style
While unknowingly beguiling
All who behold your siren's smile
While filled with envious dread
They do not roam the road
That you in beauty tread!

Yea! You walk in beauty
In the mold of mighty Aphrodite!
You guard the gate as if it were your duty
To ply the world with grace and dignity!
You stand with the ancients of ages
You're praised by prescient sages
Who yearn to enter your realm!
How and why, pray tell
Do few as you liven history's pages?
The answer cascades down from the heights of yore
Progenitor of Helen, emissary of Thor!

Poem Number 27

To Kathy

To Kathy: An Erstwhile Encounter

I was idling in place one night
When her entrance dropped jaws—
And at what cost!
My inattentive dalliance scarce let me see her,

When, thankfully, it ended, it seemed everything blended
into one—save one!
From the depths of despair she came,
Angelic presence and flair—
I fought to stymie my stare!

Next I knew, we had scaled the cloud
Of common cause—no coincidence that!
And thus we sat—for hours!
We were variously moved along
And drawn together
By fateful, fanciful, fawn!

Unsuspectingly, we entered His realm
Where we tarried 'til time for home—
I, forsooth, did *not* want to roam
Though choice had I none.
I reel as I ponder—stunned!!

Poem Number 28

Last Dance in Dedham

Last Dance in Dedham

Somehow I knew, my twirling was through
As I danced that night through two shoes!
It was a dance to end all dances, all right—
It was a sumptuous dance that lasted all night!

It's as if the gathered masses were thus enthralled
To see such a performance at the Holiday Ball
There were signs and aces and Basses on call
We stepped and leapt—through litany all!

We began our trek at the stroke of nine
The band—The Clan—was playing oh so fine!
We entered the fifties with the nifty cha-cha
We took a ride to Philly for the canine cause!

It was ten o'clock and we had not stopped!
Couples were buckling from the continuous bop—
Ricky said 'Hello' to Mary Lou—Roy gave her gifts on cue!
Johnny was singing 'Ring of Fire'—filling revelers with desire!

And we danced on! And the band played on!
If we were exhausted, we would not let on!
We, daresay, summoned strength from yesteryear—
We sang with 'Frankie'—they were very good years!

They shrank from the dance floor—one by one
'til, finally, they were gone—there remained not one!
We seized center stage—and thus did engage!
The crowd gave a din—while we donned a second wind!

We locked in step and in reminiscent gaze—
We inwardly knew we'd reached the end of our days!
Our steps slowed still, as we took the bitter pill
The last note fell—'twas the anticipated knell!

All is quiet now—as in Dedham we died
Secretly, inwardly, the years—they all cried!
It was a fitting finale to a career thus spawned
The music and laughter, though, will live on and on!

Poem Number 29

A Bad Day!

A Bad Day!

So. You think you had a bad day???
Well, let me tell you about mine!!!
Woke up at 6:00 a.m.
only to discover it wasn't me waking up in my bed!
It was somebody else who had stolen my ID!!

When I finally called 911 to have the identity thief arrested,
I dialed 800 by mistake, and got long distance information—
to Jersey, of all places!! I told them I was trying to dial 911—
they thought I said "I'm trying to find a gun!"

so they gave me the NRA!! I said "No! No! No!"
I wanted police emergency! Somebody stole my Id!
They thought I said "I'm rolling in pee!"
and gave me the emergency room! I said, "No! No!"
"No!" I'm trying to reach the police!!"

They thought I was saying, "I have leeches and fleas!"
and gave me the local veterinarian. I said "No! No! No!"
I'm trying to retrieve my identity!"
They thought I said "I'm trying to lose my virginity!"

and gave me the local whorehouse! I said "No! No!"
"No! I'm trying to find the thief who woke up in my bed!!"
I don't have to tell you what they thought I said!
That's why I'm talking with this high-pitched voice!
She had vampire teeth!! At least I solved the mystery!

No one had stolen my ID after all!
Of course they stole something else!!
Anybody seen Lorena Bobbit lately?
I gotta get back to that emergency room before it's too late!!

Poem Number 30

Street Sense

Street Sense

No one saw him make the move—cruising in last
He was *fast!*— 'twas well known—
How could he have flown so fast, from first to last?
Truth be told—nobody knows!

He was hitching horse sense to Street Sense!
He was ditching horses as though they were stable ponies—
Not his cronies!
What magnificence to this grandiose event was lent!

Kentucky! Oh Kentucky!—Have you seen such a glorious affair!
Have you seen such majesty in the air!
A spectacle fit for a Queen was seen and shared by all!
Her Majesty was there—his majesty was clear!

As gates were primed near departure time
Anxiety ruled the equine line!
Street Sense 'pared to leave the stall—
This he did as bell of the ball!

He 'peared as one whose confidence soared!
He 'peared as one who saw the score
'fore any and all, locked in a script whose ending he knew—
At quarter pole, his aim was true!

Horses on the left, horses on the right
Horses in front—but none out of sight!
He began his ascent with a burst of power
He knew full well this was his finest hour!

He had—alas!—started in arrears
This was the plan, conceived within
From conception to perception, nor failure, nor fears
His sole projection was win—only win!

And win he did!—with powerful bursts
Past mount and man—one by one!
He did not rest 'til deed was done!
He knew he had come—from last to first!

He saluted the clubhouse with a knowing glance
As he began to dance his princely prance
He celebrated early—no less his ride
His chest was heaving with well-earned pride!

Many times in life we're faced with strife
And long, imponderable odds!
Recall Street Sense and his glide inside—
You'll destroy the field like gods!

Poem Number 31

Unchecked Beauty

Unchecked Beauty

It is rare when angelic beauty reaches out and engages you
When all you wanted to do was peruse and lose yourself
In anonymity;
Fateful Ruler had other plans—
To involve our eyes in erstwhile dance
Of sweet elixir of business and concomitant caring
culled between admonitions of cycles, accounts, and balances.
How delicious the tightrope—how precarious the balance!
Until, sadly, deed was done,
Whereupon we sat in stunned silence
Ere we came crashing back to Earth!
As I touched ground, I stealthily turned around
And saw a pumpkin—I'm sure she saw a frog!

Poem Number 32

Queen Anne

Queen Anne

Has there ever been one who is more majestically beautiful than you?
Has there ever been one who represents royalty more, and style?
Has there ever been one whose inner soul is more graciously imbued
Has there ever been one whose eyes more beguile, and smile?

Has there ever been one who more by decree brings things to be?
Has there ever been one who more lends regality to the throne?
Has there ever been one who more holds in her hands life's key?
Has there ever been one whose touch is too much? No, not one!

Has there ever been one whose presence is more scintillating?
Has there ever been one whose aura, to adore her, is more golden?
Has there ever been one whose movements are more undulating?
Has there ever been one, under sun, whose spirit more emboldens?

Has there ever been one whose crown radiates more royally, I aver?
Has there ever been one whose realm overwhelms the teeming serfdom?
Has there ever been one who is more fair, as Guinevere of yesteryear?
I submit, with all that is within me—no, not one! No, not one!

Poem Number 33

The Bell Lap

The Bell Lap

"Runners take your marks!" is a stark first call
That you *must* enter the race—whether you be fleet or slow!
"Get set!" says to all to prepare to give your all
Irrevocable "Go!" starts the Starter's show!

As life is launched 'midst strength and brawn
A glance headlong gives relative position
The first lap breezes like the singing of a song
'Tis time to plan and foment your decisions!

The rhythm of the race, the setting of the pace
Occurs in a blur during the second surge!
Carefree flees amid raised, high knees
More strength is summoned from body's urge!

All doubts have flown, and you're heading home—
Race's middle mounts a formidable goal!
The prospect of rest propels you to its breast
The renewal of resolve—the beginning of the best!

Slowly slide the throttle, as all resources test
To peg what power can be generated within!
All systems are assessed—all statuses addressed
As engines swirl, ably abetted by the wind!

As third pole is passed, sweet sight is seen of home!
Bold Starter has fired his gun—'ere long will deed be done!
Time for caution has fairly flown—you're out in front alone—
This is the vaunted Bell Lap, as down the stretch you come!

Poem Number 34

Bermuda the Beautiful!

Bermuda the Beautiful!

Ay, mates! It must be seen to be believed
The fetching den of the Forty Thieves!
The pirates' cove was magically bedecked
With sirens' love 'bove shores of shipwreck!

Oh, Hamilton! Dear Hamilton! How dazzling the thrill
Of traipsing your beaches—nigh high on a hill!
A Princess you are—not even paradise a par—
I sing a song of longing—heard loudly from afar!

A dream—sweet dreams they were—of girls on Broadway
They danced and crooned—I aver—'til well the break of day!
'Twas merrily mesmerizing the magnificence of it all—
It donned the distinct feeling of a midsummer night's ball!

Alas! Then and when it was sorrowful depart
The arrow of the Archer's bow shot surely through the heart!
Flight was moot from such a shoot, so tarrying was the plan!
It was the seed of many deeds—a liaison so grand!

The isle was mine—I felt inclined—ere family was met—
The echelon was high and bronzed—my entry swiftly let!
Simon was saying—and we obeying—the call to move ahead—
The silver sand of Bermuda's land served substance for a band!

Siren—oh dear siren! I received your distant call!
It was piercing in the night—it projected light and might!
It was comely sand from shore—never seen forever more!
I heeded not your distant call—never heard forever more!

Poem Number 35

Running in Place

Running in Place

Sometimes it seems, in dreams, at night
We've simply succumbed to rabbit's plight!
Though run we try—to do or die,
Progress flies by, as mud in your eye!

The matt is well worn—confidence and care shorn!
As static stars sail by in reprise—
You ponder 'wherefore', you wonder 'maybe more'—
As fortune or fail flail relentless at your knees!

It matters not that you quicken the pace
You remain tethered to the same old place!
When you frantically force the course, you expect
That progress in relate you will get!

But, no! This is not always the case
When life dictates, for whatever reason, distaste!
It has to do, to give a clue—
With word of mouth—what you say to you!

In order to arrive at this ungainly place
Concomitant thought likely paved the way
To urge the obliging tongue to speak
To create the dastardly deed thus wreaked!

Little is needed to reverse confession
To convert vector from up to fro'
Yea! He waits in intercession
To release you from your inertial throes!

All that's needed, once you've conceded
That power to win is within—
Is resolutely state your case
"I'll win this race—not run in place!"

Poem Number 36

Trapped in a Time Warp

Trapped in a Time Warp

Before I knew it, there I was—
Dancing over Dascomb, as I gently touched down!
I knew the cause was to apply gentle gauze
To surrogate comfort, as I surveyed all around!

Further along the node, as others earthbound rode
I sensed the erstwhile presence of Robbie, and petitioned
She was a very able commander, long ago!
I inquired solicitously—not knowing my position:

"Pray tell me—does she yet navigate this crate? Is she still at the helm?"
But they could not respond—much as a specter cannot elect to
But Robbie received me, from the edge of our Galaxy
As we conversed in a language undecipherable in our realm!

In tongueless speech, she curiously beseeched:
"How came you to this place? "
"How mastered you the vastness of Space?"
"I've retired from the ire—I now live life as on a beach!"

I responded quite despondent,
"I was drawn to you, dear one!"
"We were fellow travelers eons ago!"
"How we laughed—how we funned!"

"Remember Fred? Why did you not wed?"
I recall many falls in arrears
Fred allayed all his fears
And divorced travail for a boat and a sail!

Sadly, Robbie, at his final divorce decree
There was hardly more room—daresay none left for me!
I could not enter—I could not see
Much as the condition that exists 'tween you and me!"

I find myself trapped now—lost in this warp—
I journeyed here in maudlin 'cause I craved the tepid thought!
To once again part curtain, and, smiling, take a bow—
Where are they now, Robbie—Where are you now?

Poem Number 37

Frankie's House

Frankie's House

He was *such* a little tyke—
Riding to and fro' on his bike
'Long the Mystic Valley alley—
Down the route he'd scoot each day!

This dear highway was an heirloom
'Twas like family, I wist!
Though 'twas winter, 'twas was like June
Hied us home without a hitch!

It was a winding road, I recall
With dips and knolls galore!
It felt as tall as coaster's fall
Frankie's mirth would rival a roar!

We'd pass each day on our foray
A beauteous, palatial spread!
I mused with Frankie, as we cruised the gate—
"What a handsome home, indeed!"

"One day, dear Frank, I'd like to think—
That mansion will be totally yours!
I'll inscribe your name on the window pane—
I'll emblazon your name on the doors!"

We've since departed that area erotic
Many and many eons ago!
Frankie's house, though, remains—a darling cottage
That we *yet* vow to get and bestow!

Poem Number 38

Beauty!

Beauty!

Helen! A mere face launched a thousand ships—
Sailing on high seas to retrieve her lovely liege!
Menelaus! He obsessed undying death and devotion—
Navigating undulating ocean'midst high seas!

Helen of Troy! The standard on which beauty is borne!
An equine ploy! Such elaborate ruse the world had not known!
Her irresistible gender engendered matchless passion—
Much as a queen bee directs her hapless masses!

Solomon was similarly smitten with the beautiful Queen—
He sang his soliloquies, directed by passionate desire!
He tried vainly to quench the raging pillar of fire—
Ignited by the delectable Sheba—the ravishingly beauteous being!

Marc Anthony idolized Cleopatra—she the uncannily comely and fair!
Her unassailable, sumptuous beauty mesmerized his every motion!
Life and limb would he sacrifice to entice a strand of her hair—
Yea! Her very presence plied him with unquenchable potion!

Beauty, notwithstanding, lurks in Nature similarly—
Can there be a more beautiful spectacle than the blooming of a tree?
Or the wonderful ridges and ledges, so painstakingly chiseled o'er
Carry us home, O' beautiful bridge—carry us home to roam no more!

Poem Number 39

Going Home Again!

Going Home Again!

I have been desperately sifting through the sands of time
Panning for slivers of gold in the stream of once upon a time
But all I have succeeded in finding is the fool's shell of shanties
And abandoned land launched by plans of bygone banter!

It creates a cacophony of emotion—the colliding realms of eras past!
Each venture vies for directional intent—falling forward or backward bent!
Ruminating in the library—now overgrown with rambling weeds
Walking the paths of yesterday, from which current fortune feeds!

Home has grown very quiet now, as the once—vibrant voices are gone—
Gone far from home to nestle on new sod—breaking life-long blood bonds!
If I listen, I can hear them speak to me now, across Time and Space
I can feel them beckon—as their progeny beam through in familial face!

Home, sweet home, they say, is where the wandering heart resides—
One can never feel whole—separated from his suckling mold!
It fills with chagrin the longing eye—to see in the mirror an era gone by—
We persist to reenter that realm, as a child that has outgrown his clothes!

Yes! You can go home again—as the prodigal one returning from the fields!
Unseen elements welcome and embrace you with each step—you never left!
You can hear them—if you listen! They share your breast-beating pride!
No one will notice your maudlin eye—if your long-lost child begins to cry!

Poem Number 40

The River Jordan

The River Jordan

It can be a lonely, desolate journey, if you let it.
But, it is an inevitable one, relentlessly edging ever so close to the border;
To that magnificent and grandiose symbol of human transfiguration:
The River Jordan!

It is the only journey in life that is uninterrupted, free flowing
Toward that sublime sea called Heaven, where, it, at last,
Quits its laborious trek, giving up its burdensome lading
To the white-gloved shorehands and bell boys eagerly awaiting
Their triumphant arrival—glowing!

Many trials, tribulations, and vicissitudes have beset the
solitary traveler since birth.
But even in the worst of times, God's hand is ever providing
A beacon, beckoning us back to the calm and sanctity of Mother Earth!

It, at once, leads to life's enrichment and fulfillment.
It is only necessary to guard the gates of one's heart
To ensure peace and tranquility in the sometimes double-dealing
Didactic fortunes unwittingly chosen by the unsuspecting wayfarer.

Poem Number 41

Seeds of Life

Seeds of Life

Through the heart, the mouth is fed
Life's deeds hinge on what is said!
What is pondered seeds the heart
The twain remains locked from the start!

When Fate dictates distasteful ends
In deed, they propagate from inner sins
Of hate, envy, disdain and dread
A willful welcome into your head!

If you'd like to sup at life's sweet table
If you'd like the best of which you are able
Eschew the blue and arcane thoughts
Give way to blessed give for naught!

Life and death, at tongue's behest
Are ruled by joint decree!
Things said, or good or bad
Are dispatched, and begin to be!

The thought is basic to the Book:
He spoke, and it was so!
As His progeny, He flowered
This power on Earth below!

Life, daresay, is a fertile garden
Seeds sown therein grow deeds in relate!
As they mature, grandeur, allure
May arise therefrom unabated!

Poem Number 42

Myra, My Myra

Myra, My Myra

Our meeting, dear Myra, was the talk of the town,
We whirled and twirled to melodious sounds!
The setting was hubbub and turmoil deep down—
Sonny played and swayed 'midst calls to 'get down'!

A chance encounter on the Avenue—
It seemed the moment was made for us two!
Your fair face made less of the crowd!
By charm and grace you were well endowed!

Your smile was as radiant as the sun!
Your lithesome look overruled everyone!
Never in all of my days of the past
Could I recall one with half the class!

My eyes I could not control—alas!
The elixir of you intoxicated me—fast!
I could not resist—did not want to, I wist
The call of your kiss—the fulfillment of wish!

We danced with Dave and Sam a while
We laughed along the long Broadway!
A more magnificent James Brown style
I've not seen to this very day!

All good things, they cannot last!
The time for the party had sadly passed!
I looked around, and there was Ed—
Ol' Granddad had gotten to his head!

I could not leave him prey to Time—
He had not willingly succumbed to wine!
It was the Adversary egging him on—
I said, "Let's go, Ed!" and we three were gone!

We assured that he was home, all right
Whereupon our taxi resumed its flight!
Next, we parted in Shakespearean tone—
And I was forthwith all alone!

Our friendship flourished, for brief interlude
'til tragedy struck, akin to Romeo and Jule'
I know not where she is this day—
She tried desperately to lead the way!

But follow I wouldn't—who knows why?
The untamed whims of youth, I sigh!
She wanted to merge, and began to cry—
Myra, my Myra, please dry your eye!

Poem Number 43

Teresa's Lament

Teresa's Lament
(A Poem for Teresa—Who Adored Me)

It was last millennium that last
I spanned this grand land—unsurpassed
In grandeur, splendor, dreams, and streams
Flung forward, unrelenting, pursuing that dream
That was old—yet new!
It was nineteen seventy-two!
I was wrapped in rolling green!
I soared, ever forward, leaving Time, it seemed!
It was a journey into unknowing night.
I swear I crossed the Divide—what a fright!
My senses seared from the exposed cold!
It was hours before I recaptured my soul—
Only to deliver to Teri bittersweet dole!
The water from her weeping, pain, and worry
Gave little cause to pause those days—
It could not part the heart of granite ways
Of youth! It changed, forsooth, us forever!
Never again would that great expanse—the great Divide
Collapse around my Teresa and me
And cause the laws of Time to flee!
Oh! What we'd give to again be that free—
Bound together—tethered—through Eternity!

Poem Number 44

You're Nobody 'til Somebody Wants You!

You're Nobody 'til Somebody Wants You!

Sitting by the phone—sitting all alone!
You're nobody 'til somebody wants you
Sitting with a pole—deep into the hole!
You're nobody 'til somebody wants you!

As sudden as you please—A ring! A ring! Oh please!
You're nobody 'til somebody wants you!
The pole gives a jerk—You have one in the lurch!
You're nobody 'til somebody wants you!

It's Peggy Lou, who vowed to coo!
You're nobody 'til somebody wants you!
"It's been a while—How do you do!"
You're nobody 'til somebody wants you!

In mid phone call, wait comes to call!
You're nobody 'til somebody wants you!
"It's Barbara Ann—Hey what's the plan!"
You're nobody 'til somebody wants you!

"Hold on, sweet one—I'm under the gun!"
You're nobody 'til somebody wants you
"Hey Peggy Sue—I'll return to you!"
You're nobody 'til somebody wants you!

"Hey Barbara Ann—Let's kick some sand"!
You're nobody 'til somebody wants you!
But line is dead! Oh drat! Oh dread!
You're nobody 'til somebody wants you!

"Sweet Peggy Sue—I do love you"!
You're nobody 'til somebody wants you!
"Love me, Dan?—Was that Barbara Ann?"
You're nobody 'til somebody wants you!

Back by the phone—in insular home!
You're nobody 'til somebody wants you!
You won't get a ring 'til sometime mid spring!
You're nobody 'til somebody wants you!

Poem Number 45

Whistling in the Wind

Whistling in the Wind

When furor begins, so does the wind
When one whistles, does it return within!
When you whistle in the wind, can it nonetheless be heard?
When you whistle in the wind, do you sail like a bird?

When you whistle in the wind, are your thoughts as pure as gold?
When you whistle in the wind, can your innermost be told?
Can you shrill the whip-or-will's singular song?
Can you quote his rote all day long?

When there are thoughts deep down that portend a frown
Divert them and insert for them a trill!
Even when no one—not a soul—can be found
Reverse them and thereby flower your will!

When you whistle in the wind, and no one is around
Can one hear you making music?—Does your music make a sound?
I remit to you the answer—it's as clear as ocean blue—
Whistling is indeed God's salve, applied inside to you!

Poem Number 46

Giving Your All

Giving Your All (To Frankie)

Greater love has no one
Than when he gives *one*—and then he has none!
He depends on Providence to recompense
He denies himself his natural sense!

Giving when in need is as alms in kind
Giving when in need is like sight to the blind!
When you have battled 'midst prattle and contend
When Nature's First Law is merely words in the end!

You side with the Angels to minister here on Earth
You execute His mission though you yourself in dearth!
You give material manifest to God's almighty plan—
You simply transmit the energy supplied by His own hand!

You fight the good fight—you strive day and night!
You never succumb to odds—whatever the plight!
When fireworks flare—from ferocious firefights
Glorious victory is seldom far from sight!

When you've given your all, you've built up treasure
When you've nothing left to burn, return is given full measure!
You cannot match this priceless gift—
God give you grace—and holy shrift!

Poem Number 47

A Birthday Prayer for My Love

A Birthday Prayer for My Love

Dear God, my love has petitioned the Court of High Praise
For bounteous blessings and deliverance from self-imposed malaise!
He asks that you guide him each and every day—
In all that he does—in all that he says!

He asks that you be—as you said in your Book
His breastplate and buckler—a totally warlike look!
For he knows we're engaged in fighting the demonic clan—
He knows you will sustain him—until the bitter end!

Your exploits as Supreme Commander are, indeed, non-pareill!
You've plundered the forces of evil—you've sealed the gates of Hell!
On each and every avenue that we have yet to travel
You've clearly marked the territory—recorded it with gavel!

He sits now 'neath your Kingly throne, as subject, supplicating
He importunes you, as subjects do, to end his inundating,
To give him favor, surcease from labor, O Father, for this I pray—
To give sweet ease, and Heavenly keys, each step along the way!

Poem Number 48

Long Distance Roses

Long Distance Roses

They send a lovely scent, these odiferous emissaries of love!
Transfigured by the wind, giving substance to bent!
It matters not the time when these petals are thusly lent—
Fair flowering from Above—love showering as a dove!

In torrid times of delayed days and far-flung forays
It gives pause to gracious gatherings and heartfelt gratifications
Many be there days where suckling sorrow soars
For want of roses—salve to assuage life's inundations!

It has many names, this many-splendored charming bloom—
Love, Peace, Trust, Beauty—as many as can fill a room!
In the end, its name is moot—what it does will follow suit!
God-given gilded gift, plying plant with deep down roots!

When inadvertent duties at times impede your homeward flight
When absent your love's arms, you must dream on in the night
Long distance roses manifest your intended destination!
Nature's tongue makes you as one—a heavenly florid libation!

Poem Number 49

A Valentine of Fine Wine

A Valentine of Fine Wine

As grapes grow from rich soil
So life and love grow—amid turbulence and toil
Buttressed by fortresses of fire and fortitude,
Composed by the Great Master—eclectic etudes
As our glowing Star fuels from afar
Our mundane pursuits,
Love eternal springs and sings
Its annual red ritual, as sung by Cupid.

You are the Star, shining o'er the Sea of Tranquility
You are the light, illuminating the stage
where we ply our art;
I loved you from the start
Its life as light from the Sun!

Poem Number 50

The Fan

The Fan

The fan will follow the object of his adoration, regardless
The fan will come to the park in thunder, rain or darkness
The fan is not deterred by mere disparity or vicissitude
The fan will love when all else is moot!

The fan is not given to outbursts of ire!
The fan will respond always in dire!
The fan will smile while tables are turning—
He'll even beguile while Rome is burning!

He'll cheer you on when hope is thin—
He'll will you to that elusive win!
He'll lift you up when chin is down—
He'll pick you up when knocked to the ground!

I am your true and staunchest fan!
I lead by deed your serfdom—by decree!
You say as well you're mine? Pray tell!!
We admire each other mutually!

Printed in the United States
200500BV00004B/187/A